THIS JOURNAL BELONGS TO

Name:_____

Address:_____

_____

Phone:_____ Cell:_____

email:_____

MMEGA PUBLISHING 2019
Cover: OpenClipart-Vectors from PixabayImages from Pixabay

A

Name_____
Street Address_____
City:_____State:____Zip Code:_____
Home Phone:_____Cell Phone:_____
Work Phone:_____Email:_____
Notes:

Name_____
Street Address_____
City:_____State:____Zip Code:_____
Home Phone:_____Cell Phone:_____
Work Phone:_____Email:_____
Notes:

Name_____
Street Address_____
City:_____State:____Zip Code:_____
Home Phone:_____Cell Phone:_____
Work Phone:_____Email:_____
Notes:

Name_____
Street Address_____
City:_____State:____Zip Code:_____
Home Phone:_____Cell Phone:_____
Work Phone:_____Email:_____
Notes:

Comments:

Address Book   A

Name_____
Street Address_____
City:_____**State:**____**Zip Code:**_____
Home Phone:_____**Cell Phone:**_____
Work Phone:_____**Email:**_____
Notes:

Name_____
Street Address_____
City:_____**State:**____**Zip Code:**_____
Home Phone:_____**Cell Phone:**_____
Work Phone:_____**Email:**_____
Notes:

Name_____
Street Address_____
City:_____**State:**____**Zip Code:**_____
Home Phone:_____**Cell Phone:**_____
Work Phone:_____**Email:**_____
Notes:

Name_____
Street Address_____
City:_____**State:**____**Zip Code:**_____
Home Phone:_____**Cell Phone:**_____
Work Phone:_____**Email:**_____
Notes:

Comments:

Name_____

Street Address_____

City:_____**State:**____**Zip Code:**_____

Home Phone:_____**Cell Phone:**_____

Work Phone:_____**Email:**_____

Notes:

Name_____

Street Address_____

City:_____**State:**____**Zip Code:**_____

Home Phone:_____**Cell Phone:**_____

Work Phone:_____**Email:**_____

Notes:

Name_____

Street Address_____

City:_____**State:**____**Zip Code:**_____

Home Phone:_____**Cell Phone:**_____

Work Phone:_____**Email:**_____

Notes:

Name_____

Street Address_____

City:_____**State:**____**Zip Code:**_____

Home Phone:_____**Cell Phone:**_____

Work Phone:_____**Email:**_____

Notes:

Comments:

Address Book   A

Name_____
Street Address_____
City:_____State:____Zip Code:_____
Home Phone:_____Cell Phone:_____
Work Phone:_____Email:_____
Notes:

Name_____
Street Address_____
City:_____State:____Zip Code:_____
Home Phone:_____Cell Phone:_____
Work Phone:_____Email:_____
Notes:

Name_____
Street Address_____
City:_____State:____Zip Code:_____
Home Phone:_____Cell Phone:_____
Work Phone:_____Email:_____
Notes:

Name_____
Street Address_____
City:_____State:____Zip Code:_____
Home Phone:_____Cell Phone:_____
Work Phone:_____Email:_____
Notes:

Comments:

Name_____

Street Address_____

City:_____**State:**____**Zip Code:**_____

Home Phone:_____**Cell Phone:**_____

Work Phone:_____**Email:**_____

Notes:

Name_____

Street Address_____

City:_____**State:**____**Zip Code:**_____

Home Phone:_____**Cell Phone:**_____

Work Phone:_____**Email:**_____

Notes:

Name_____

Street Address_____

City:_____**State:**____**Zip Code:**_____

Home Phone:_____**Cell Phone:**_____

Work Phone:_____**Email:**_____

Notes:

Name_____

Street Address_____

City:_____**State:**____**Zip Code:**_____

Home Phone:_____**Cell Phone:**_____

Work Phone:_____**Email:**_____

Notes:

Comments:

Address Book   B

Name_____

Street Address_____

City:_____State:____Zip Code:_____

Home Phone:_____Cell Phone:_____

Work Phone:_____Email:_____

Notes:

Name_____

Street Address_____

City:_____State:____Zip Code:_____

Home Phone:_____Cell Phone:_____

Work Phone:_____Email:_____

Notes:

Name_____

Street Address_____

City:_____State:____Zip Code:_____

Home Phone:_____Cell Phone:_____

Work Phone:_____Email:_____

Notes:

Name_____

Street Address_____

City:_____State:____Zip Code:_____

Home Phone:_____Cell Phone:_____

Work Phone:_____Email:_____

Notes:

Comments:

Name_____
Street Address_____
City:_____**State:**_____**Zip Code:**_____
Home Phone:_____**Cell Phone:**_____
Work Phone:_____**Email:**_____
Notes:

Name_____
Street Address_____
City:_____**State:**_____**Zip Code:**_____
Home Phone:_____**Cell Phone:**_____
Work Phone:_____**Email:**_____
Notes:

Name_____
Street Address_____
City:_____**State:**_____**Zip Code:**_____
Home Phone:_____**Cell Phone:**_____
Work Phone:_____**Email:**_____
Notes:

Name_____
Street Address_____
City:_____**State:**_____**Zip Code:**_____
Home Phone:_____**Cell Phone:**_____
Work Phone:_____**Email:**_____
Notes:

Comments:

Address Book   B

Name_____

Street Address_____

City:_____**State:**____**Zip Code:**_____

Home Phone:_____**Cell Phone:**_____

Work Phone:_____**Email:**_____

Notes:

Name_____

Street Address_____

City:_____**State:**____**Zip Code:**_____

Home Phone:_____**Cell Phone:**_____

Work Phone:_____**Email:**_____

Notes:

Name_____

Street Address_____

City:_____**State:**____**Zip Code:**_____

Home Phone:_____**Cell Phone:**_____

Work Phone:_____**Email:**_____

Notes:

Name_____

Street Address_____

City:_____**State:**____**Zip Code:**_____

Home Phone:_____**Cell Phone:**_____

Work Phone:_____**Email:**_____

Notes:

Comments:

Name_____
Street Address_____
City:_____**State:**____**Zip Code:**_____
Home Phone:_____**Cell Phone:**_____
Work Phone:_____**Email:**_____
Notes:

Name_____
Street Address_____
City:_____**State:**____**Zip Code:**_____
Home Phone:_____**Cell Phone:**_____
Work Phone:_____**Email:**_____
Notes:

Name_____
Street Address_____
City:_____**State:**____**Zip Code:**_____
Home Phone:_____**Cell Phone:**_____
Work Phone:_____**Email:**_____
Notes:

Name_____
Street Address_____
City:_____**State:**____**Zip Code:**_____
Home Phone:_____**Cell Phone:**_____
Work Phone:_____**Email:**_____
Notes:

Comments:

Address Book   C

Name_____

Street Address_____

City:_____**State:**____**Zip Code:**_____

Home Phone:_____**Cell Phone:**_____

Work Phone:_____**Email:**_____

Notes:

Name_____

Street Address_____

City:_____**State:**____**Zip Code:**_____

Home Phone:_____**Cell Phone:**_____

Work Phone:_____**Email:**_____

Notes:

Name_____

Street Address_____

City:_____**State:**____**Zip Code:**_____

Home Phone:_____**Cell Phone:**_____

Work Phone:_____**Email:**_____

Notes:

Name_____

Street Address_____

City:_____**State:**____**Zip Code:**_____

Home Phone:_____**Cell Phone:**_____

Work Phone:_____**Email:**_____

Notes:

Comments:

Name_____

Street Address_____

City:_____**State:**____**Zip Code:**_____

Home Phone:_____**Cell Phone:**_____

Work Phone:_____**Email:**_____

Notes:

Name_____

Street Address_____

City:_____**State:**____**Zip Code:**_____

Home Phone:_____**Cell Phone:**_____

Work Phone:_____**Email:**_____

Notes:

Name_____

Street Address_____

City:_____**State:**____**Zip Code:**_____

Home Phone:_____**Cell Phone:**_____

Work Phone:_____**Email:**_____

Notes:

Name_____

Street Address_____

City:_____**State:**____**Zip Code:**_____

Home Phone:_____**Cell Phone:**_____

Work Phone:_____**Email:**_____

Notes:

Comments:

Address Book   C

Name_____
Street Address_____
City:_____State:____Zip Code:_____
Home Phone:_____Cell Phone:_____
Work Phone:_____Email:_____
Notes:

Name_____
Street Address_____
City:_____State:____Zip Code:_____
Home Phone:_____Cell Phone:_____
Work Phone:_____Email:_____
Notes:

Name_____
Street Address_____
City:_____State:____Zip Code:_____
Home Phone:_____Cell Phone:_____
Work Phone:_____Email:_____
Notes:

Name_____
Street Address_____
City:_____State:____Zip Code:_____
Home Phone:_____Cell Phone:_____
Work Phone:_____Email:_____
Notes:

Comments:

Name_____

Street Address_____

City:_____**State:**_____**Zip Code:**_____

Home Phone:_____**Cell Phone:**_____

Work Phone:_____**Email:**_____

Notes:

Name_____

Street Address_____

City:_____**State:**_____**Zip Code:**_____

Home Phone:_____**Cell Phone:**_____

Work Phone:_____**Email:**_____

Notes:

Name_____

Street Address_____

City:_____**State:**_____**Zip Code:**_____

Home Phone:_____**Cell Phone:**_____

Work Phone:_____**Email:**_____

Notes:

Name_____

Street Address_____

City:_____**State:**_____**Zip Code:**_____

Home Phone:_____**Cell Phone:**_____

Work Phone:_____**Email:**_____

Notes:

Comments:

Address Book   D

Name_____
Street Address_____
City:_____State:____Zip Code:_____
Home Phone:_____Cell Phone:_____
Work Phone:_____Email:_____
Notes:

Name_____
Street Address_____
City:_____State:____Zip Code:_____
Home Phone:_____Cell Phone:_____
Work Phone:_____Email:_____
Notes:

Name_____
Street Address_____
City:_____State:____Zip Code:_____
Home Phone:_____Cell Phone:_____
Work Phone:_____Email:_____
Notes:

Name_____
Street Address_____
City:_____State:____Zip Code:_____
Home Phone:_____Cell Phone:_____
Work Phone:_____Email:_____
Notes:

Comments:

Name_____
Street Address_____
City:_____**State:**____**Zip Code:**_____
Home Phone:_____**Cell Phone:**_____
Work Phone:_____**Email:**_____
Notes:

Name_____
Street Address_____
City:_____**State:**____**Zip Code:**_____
Home Phone:_____**Cell Phone:**_____
Work Phone:_____**Email:**_____
Notes:

Name_____
Street Address_____
City:_____**State:**____**Zip Code:**_____
Home Phone:_____**Cell Phone:**_____
Work Phone:_____**Email:**_____
Notes:

Name_____
Street Address_____
City:_____**State:**____**Zip Code:**_____
Home Phone:_____**Cell Phone:**_____
Work Phone:_____**Email:**_____
Notes:

Comments:

Address Book   D

Name_____
Street Address_____
City:_____**State:**____**Zip Code:**_____
Home Phone:_____**Cell Phone:**_____
Work Phone:_____**Email:**_____
Notes:

Name_____
Street Address_____
City:_____**State:**____**Zip Code:**_____
Home Phone:_____**Cell Phone:**_____
Work Phone:_____**Email:**_____
Notes:

Name_____
Street Address_____
City:_____**State:**____**Zip Code:**_____
Home Phone:_____**Cell Phone:**_____
Work Phone:_____**Email:**_____
Notes:

Name_____
Street Address_____
City:_____**State:**____**Zip Code:**_____
Home Phone:_____**Cell Phone:**_____
Work Phone:_____**Email:**_____
Notes:

Comments:

Name_____

Street Address_____

City:_____ **State:**____ **Zip Code:**_____

Home Phone:_____ **Cell Phone:**_____

Work Phone:_____ **Email:**_____

Notes:

Name_____

Street Address_____

City:_____ **State:**____ **Zip Code:**_____

Home Phone:_____ **Cell Phone:**_____

Work Phone:_____ **Email:**_____

Notes:

Name_____

Street Address_____

City:_____ **State:**____ **Zip Code:**_____

Home Phone:_____ **Cell Phone:**_____

Work Phone:_____ **Email:**_____

Notes:

Name_____

Street Address_____

City:_____ **State:**____ **Zip Code:**_____

Home Phone:_____ **Cell Phone:**_____

Work Phone:_____ **Email:**_____

Notes:

Comments:

Name_____

Street Address_____

City:_____**State:**____**Zip Code:**_____

Home Phone:_____**Cell Phone:**_____

Work Phone:_____**Email:**_____

Notes:

Name_____

Street Address_____

City:_____**State:**____**Zip Code:**_____

Home Phone:_____**Cell Phone:**_____

Work Phone:_____**Email:**_____

Notes:

Name_____

Street Address_____

City:_____**State:**____**Zip Code:**_____

Home Phone:_____**Cell Phone:**_____

Work Phone:_____**Email:**_____

Notes:

Name_____

Street Address_____

City:_____**State:**____**Zip Code:**_____

Home Phone:_____**Cell Phone:**_____

Work Phone:_____**Email:**_____

Notes:

Comments:

E	Address Book

Name_____
Street Address_____
City:_____**State:**____**Zip Code:**_____
Home Phone:_____**Cell Phone:**_____
Work Phone:_____**Email:**_____
Notes:

Name_____
Street Address_____
City:_____**State:**____**Zip Code:**_____
Home Phone:_____**Cell Phone:**_____
Work Phone:_____**Email:**_____
Notes:

Name_____
Street Address_____
City:_____**State:**____**Zip Code:**_____
Home Phone:_____**Cell Phone:**_____
Work Phone:_____**Email:**_____
Notes:

Name_____
Street Address_____
City:_____**State:**____**Zip Code:**_____
Home Phone:_____**Cell Phone:**_____
Work Phone:_____**Email:**_____
Notes:

Comments:

Address Book   E

Name_____

Street Address_____

City:_____**State:**____**Zip Code:**_____

Home Phone:_____**Cell Phone:**_____

Work Phone:_____**Email:**_____

Notes:

Name_____

Street Address_____

City:_____**State:**____**Zip Code:**_____

Home Phone:_____**Cell Phone:**_____

Work Phone:_____**Email:**_____

Notes:

Name_____

Street Address_____

City:_____**State:**____**Zip Code:**_____

Home Phone:_____**Cell Phone:**_____

Work Phone:_____**Email:**_____

Notes:

Name_____

Street Address_____

City:_____**State:**____**Zip Code:**_____

Home Phone:_____**Cell Phone:**_____

Work Phone:_____**Email:**_____

Notes:

Comments:

Name_____

Street Address_____

City:_____**State:**_____**Zip Code:**_____

Home Phone:_____**Cell Phone:**_____

Work Phone:_____**Email:**_____

Notes:

Name_____

Street Address_____

City:_____**State:**_____**Zip Code:**_____

Home Phone:_____**Cell Phone:**_____

Work Phone:_____**Email:**_____

Notes:

Name_____

Street Address_____

City:_____**State:**_____**Zip Code:**_____

Home Phone:_____**Cell Phone:**_____

Work Phone:_____**Email:**_____

Notes:

Name_____

Street Address_____

City:_____**State:**_____**Zip Code:**_____

Home Phone:_____ **Cell Phone:**_____

Work Phone:_____**Email:**_____

Notes:

Comments:

Address Book   F

Name_____
Street Address_____
City:_____**State:**____**Zip Code:**_____
Home Phone:_____**Cell Phone:**_____
Work Phone:_____**Email:**_____
Notes:

Name_____
Street Address_____
City:_____**State:**____**Zip Code:**_____
Home Phone:_____**Cell Phone:**_____
Work Phone:_____**Email:**_____
Notes:

Name_____
Street Address_____
City:_____**State:**____**Zip Code:**_____
Home Phone:_____**Cell Phone:**_____
Work Phone:_____**Email:**_____
Notes:

Name_____
Street Address_____
City:_____**State:**____**Zip Code:**_____
Home Phone:_____**Cell Phone:**_____
Work Phone:_____**Email:**_____
Notes:

Comments:

F   **Address Book**

Name_____
Street Address_____
City:_____**State:**____**Zip Code:**_____
Home Phone:_____**Cell Phone:**_____
Work Phone:_____**Email:**_____
Notes:

Name_____
Street Address_____
City:_____**State:**____**Zip Code:**_____
Home Phone:_____**Cell Phone:**_____
Work Phone:_____**Email:**_____
Notes:

Name_____
Street Address_____
City:_____**State:**____**Zip Code:**_____
Home Phone:_____**Cell Phone:**_____
Work Phone:_____**Email:**_____
Notes:

Name_____
Street Address_____
City:_____**State:**____**Zip Code:**_____
Home Phone:_____**Cell Phone:**_____
Work Phone:_____**Email:**_____
Notes:

Comments:

Address Book   F

Name_____

Street Address_____

City:_____**State:**____**Zip Code:**_____

Home Phone:_____**Cell Phone:**_____

Work Phone:_____**Email:**_____

Notes:

Name_____

Street Address_____

City:_____**State:**____**Zip Code:**_____

Home Phone:_____**Cell Phone:**_____

Work Phone:_____**Email:**_____

Notes:

Name_____

Street Address_____

City:_____**State:**____**Zip Code:**_____

Home Phone:_____**Cell Phone:**_____

Work Phone:_____**Email:**_____

Notes:

Name_____

Street Address_____

City:_____**State:**____**Zip Code:**_____

Home Phone:_____**Cell Phone:**_____

Work Phone:_____**Email:**_____

Notes:

Comments:

Name_____

Street Address_____

City:_____**State:**____**Zip Code:**_____

Home Phone:_____**Cell Phone:**_____

Work Phone:_____**Email:**_____

Notes:

Name_____

Street Address_____

City:_____**State:**____**Zip Code:**_____

Home Phone:_____**Cell Phone:**_____

Work Phone:_____**Email:**_____

Notes:

Name_____

Street Address_____

City:_____**State:**____**Zip Code:**_____

Home Phone:_____**Cell Phone:**_____

Work Phone:_____**Email:**_____

Notes:

Name_____

Street Address_____

City:_____**State:**____**Zip Code:**_____

Home Phone:_____**Cell Phone:**_____

Work Phone:_____**Email:**_____

Notes:

Comments:

Address Book   G

Name_____

Street Address_____

City:_____**State:**____**Zip Code:**_____

Home Phone:_____**Cell Phone:**_____

Work Phone:_____**Email:**_____

Notes:

Name_____

Street Address_____

City:_____**State:**____**Zip Code:**_____

Home Phone:_____**Cell Phone:**_____

Work Phone:_____**Email:**_____

Notes:

Name_____

Street Address_____

City:_____**State:**____**Zip Code:**_____

Home Phone:_____**Cell Phone:**_____

Work Phone:_____**Email:**_____

Notes:

Name_____

Street Address_____

City:_____**State:**____**Zip Code:**_____

Home Phone:_____**Cell Phone:**_____

Work Phone:_____**Email:**_____

Notes:

Comments:

Name_____

Street Address_____

City:_____**State:**____**Zip Code:**_____

Home Phone:_____**Cell Phone:**_____

Work Phone:_____**Email:**_____

Notes:

Name_____

Street Address_____

City:_____**State:**____**Zip Code:**_____

Home Phone:_____**Cell Phone:**_____

Work Phone:_____**Email:**_____

Notes:

Name_____

Street Address_____

City:_____**State:**____**Zip Code:**_____

Home Phone:_____**Cell Phone:**_____

Work Phone:_____**Email:**_____

Notes:

Name_____

Street Address_____

City:_____**State:**____**Zip Code:**_____

Home Phone:_____**Cell Phone:**_____

Work Phone:_____**Email:**_____

Notes:

Comments:

Address Book   G

Name_____

Street Address_____

City:_____**State:**____**Zip Code:**_____

Home Phone:_____**Cell Phone:**_____

Work Phone:_____**Email:**_____

Notes:

Name_____

Street Address_____

City:_____**State:**____**Zip Code:**_____

Home Phone:_____**Cell Phone:**_____

Work Phone:_____**Email:**_____

Notes:

Name_____

Street Address_____

City:_____**State:**____**Zip Code:**_____

Home Phone:_____**Cell Phone:**_____

Work Phone:_____**Email:**_____

Notes:

Name_____

Street Address_____

City:_____**State:**____**Zip Code:**_____

Home Phone:_____**Cell Phone:**_____

Work Phone:_____**Email:**_____

Notes:

Comments:

Name_____

Street Address_____

City:_____**State:**____**Zip Code:**_____

Home Phone:_____**Cell Phone:**_____

Work Phone:_____**Email:**_____

Notes:

Name_____

Street Address_____

City:_____**State:**____**Zip Code:**_____

Home Phone:_____**Cell Phone:**_____

Work Phone:_____**Email:**_____

Notes:

Name_____

Street Address_____

City:_____**State:**____**Zip Code:**_____

Home Phone:_____**Cell Phone:**_____

Work Phone:_____**Email:**_____

Notes:

Name_____

Street Address_____

City:_____**State:**____**Zip Code:**_____

Home Phone:_____**Cell Phone:**_____

Work Phone:_____**Email:**_____

Notes:

Comments:

Address Book   H

Name_____
Street Address_____
City:_____**State:**____**Zip Code:**_____
Home Phone:_____**Cell Phone:**_____
Work Phone:_____**Email:**_____
Notes:

Name_____
Street Address_____
City:_____**State:**____**Zip Code:**_____
Home Phone:_____**Cell Phone:**_____
Work Phone:_____**Email:**_____
Notes:

Name_____
Street Address_____
City:_____**State:**____**Zip Code:**_____
Home Phone:_____**Cell Phone:**_____
Work Phone:_____**Email:**_____
Notes:

Name_____
Street Address_____
City:_____**State:**____**Zip Code:**_____
Home Phone:_____**Cell Phone:**_____
Work Phone:_____**Email:**_____
Notes:

Comments:

Name_____

Street Address_____

City:_____**State:**____**Zip Code:**_____

Home Phone:_____**Cell Phone:**_____

Work Phone:_____**Email:**_____

Notes:

Name_____

Street Address_____

City:_____**State:**____**Zip Code:**_____

Home Phone:_____**Cell Phone:**_____

Work Phone:_____**Email:**_____

Notes:

Name_____

Street Address_____

City:_____**State:**____**Zip Code:**_____

Home Phone:_____**Cell Phone:**_____

Work Phone:_____**Email:**_____

Notes:

Name_____

Street Address_____

City:_____**State:**____**Zip Code:**_____

Home Phone:_____**Cell Phone:**_____

Work Phone:_____**Email:**_____

Notes:

Comments:

Address Book   H

Name_____

Street Address_____

City:_____**State:**____**Zip Code:**_____

Home Phone:_____**Cell Phone:**_____

Work Phone:_____**Email:**_____

Notes:

Name_____

Street Address_____

City:_____**State:**____**Zip Code:**_____

Home Phone:_____**Cell Phone:**_____

Work Phone:_____**Email:**_____

Notes:

Name_____

Street Address_____

City:_____**State:**____**Zip Code:**_____

Home Phone:_____**Cell Phone:**_____

Work Phone:_____**Email:**_____

Notes:

Name_____

Street Address_____

City:_____**State:**____**Zip Code:**_____

Home Phone:_____**Cell Phone:**_____

Work Phone:_____**Email:**_____

Notes:

Comments:

Name_____

Street Address_____

City:_____**State:**____**Zip Code:**_____

Home Phone:_____**Cell Phone:**_____

Work Phone:_____**Email:**_____

Notes:

Name_____

Street Address_____

City:_____**State:**____**Zip Code:**_____

Home Phone:_____**Cell Phone:**_____

Work Phone:_____**Email:**_____

Notes:

Name_____

Street Address_____

City:_____**State:**____**Zip Code:**_____

Home Phone:_____**Cell Phone:**_____

Work Phone:_____**Email:**_____

Notes:

Name_____

Street Address_____

City:_____**State:**____**Zip Code:**_____

Home Phone:_____**Cell Phone:**_____

Work Phone:_____**Email:**_____

Notes:

Comments:

Address Book   I

Name_____

Street Address_____

City:_____**State:**____**Zip Code:**_____

Home Phone:_____**Cell Phone:**_____

Work Phone:_____**Email:**_____

Notes:

Name_____

Street Address_____

City:_____**State:**____**Zip Code:**_____

Home Phone:_____**Cell Phone:**_____

Work Phone:_____**Email:**_____

Notes:

Name_____

Street Address_____

City:_____**State:**____**Zip Code:**_____

Home Phone:_____**Cell Phone:**_____

Work Phone:_____**Email:**_____

Notes:

Name_____

Street Address_____

City:_____**State:**____**Zip Code:**_____

Home Phone:_____**Cell Phone:**_____

Work Phone:_____**Email:**_____

Notes:

Comments:

Name_____

Street Address_____

City:_____**State:**_____**Zip Code:**_____

Home Phone:_____**Cell Phone:**_____

Work Phone:_____**Email:**_____

Notes:

Name_____

Street Address_____

City:_____**State:**_____**Zip Code:**_____

Home Phone:_____**Cell Phone:**_____

Work Phone:_____**Email:**_____

Notes:

Name_____

Street Address_____

City:_____**State:**_____**Zip Code:**_____

Home Phone:_____**Cell Phone:**_____

Work Phone:_____**Email:**_____

Notes:

Name_____

Street Address_____

City:_____**State:**_____**Zip Code:**_____

Home Phone:_____**Cell Phone:**_____

Work Phone:_____**Email:**_____

Notes:

Comments:

Address Book   I

Name_____
Street Address_____
City:_____State:____Zip Code:_____
Home Phone:_____Cell Phone:_____
Work Phone:_____Email:_____
Notes:

Name_____
Street Address_____
City:_____State:____Zip Code:_____
Home Phone:_____Cell Phone:_____
Work Phone:_____Email:_____
Notes:

Name_____
Street Address_____
City:_____State:____Zip Code:_____
Home Phone:_____Cell Phone:_____
Work Phone:_____Email:_____
Notes:

Name_____
Street Address_____
City:_____State:____Zip Code:_____
Home Phone:_____Cell Phone:_____
Work Phone:_____Email:_____
Notes:

Comments:

Name_____

Street Address_____

City:_____**State:**____**Zip Code:**_____

Home Phone:_____**Cell Phone:**_____

Work Phone:_____**Email:**_____

Notes:

Name_____

Street Address_____

City:_____**State:**____**Zip Code:**_____

Home Phone:_____**Cell Phone:**_____

Work Phone:_____**Email:**_____

Notes:

Name_____

Street Address_____

City:_____**State:**____**Zip Code:**_____

Home Phone:_____**Cell Phone:**_____

Work Phone:_____**Email:**_____

Notes:

Name_____

Street Address_____

City:_____**State:**____**Zip Code:**_____

Home Phone:_____**Cell Phone:**_____

Work Phone:_____**Email:**_____

Notes:

Comments:

Address Book   J

Name_____

Street Address_____

City:_____**State:**____**Zip Code:**_____

Home Phone:_____**Cell Phone:**_____

Work Phone:_____**Email:**_____

Notes:

Name_____

Street Address_____

City:_____**State:**____**Zip Code:**_____

Home Phone:_____**Cell Phone:**_____

Work Phone:_____**Email:**_____

Notes:

Name_____

Street Address_____

City:_____**State:**____**Zip Code:**_____

Home Phone:_____**Cell Phone:**_____

Work Phone:_____**Email:**_____

Notes:

Name_____

Street Address_____

City:_____**State:**____**Zip Code:**_____

Home Phone:_____**Cell Phone:**_____

Work Phone:_____**Email:**_____

Notes:

Comments:

Name_____

Street Address_____

City:_____**State:**____**Zip Code:**_____

Home Phone:_____**Cell Phone:**_____

Work Phone:_____**Email:**_____

Notes:

Name_____

Street Address_____

City:_____**State:**____**Zip Code:**_____

Home Phone:_____**Cell Phone:**_____

Work Phone:_____**Email:**_____

Notes:

Name_____

Street Address_____

City:_____**State:**____**Zip Code:**_____

Home Phone:_____**Cell Phone:**_____

Work Phone:_____**Email:**_____

Notes:

Name_____

Street Address_____

City:_____**State:**____**Zip Code:**_____

Home Phone:_____**Cell Phone:**_____

Work Phone:_____**Email:**_____

Notes:

Comments:

Address Book   J

Name_____

Street Address_____

City:_____**State:**____**Zip Code:**_____

Home Phone:_____**Cell Phone:**_____

Work Phone:_____**Email:**_____

Notes:

Name_____

Street Address_____

City:_____**State:**____**Zip Code:**_____

Home Phone:_____**Cell Phone:**_____

Work Phone:_____**Email:**_____

Notes:

Name_____

Street Address_____

City:_____**State:**____**Zip Code:**_____

Home Phone:_____**Cell Phone:**_____

Work Phone:_____**Email:**_____

Notes:

Name_____

Street Address_____

City:_____**State:**____**Zip Code:**_____

Home Phone:_____**Cell Phone:**_____

Work Phone:_____**Email:**_____

Notes:

Comments:

Name_____

Street Address_____

City:_____**State:**____**Zip Code:**_____

Home Phone:_____**Cell Phone:**_____

Work Phone:_____**Email:**_____

Notes:

Name_____

Street Address_____

City:_____**State:**____**Zip Code:**_____

Home Phone:_____**Cell Phone:**_____

Work Phone:_____**Email:**_____

Notes:

Name_____

Street Address_____

City:_____**State:**____**Zip Code:**_____

Home Phone:_____**Cell Phone:**_____

Work Phone:_____**Email:**_____

Notes:

Name_____

Street Address_____

City:_____**State:**____**Zip Code:**_____

Home Phone:_____**Cell Phone:**_____

Work Phone:_____**Email:**_____

Notes:

Comments:

Address Book   K

Name_____
Street Address_____
City:_____**State:**_____**Zip Code:**_____
Home Phone:_____**Cell Phone:**_____
Work Phone:_____**Email:**_____
Notes:

Name_____
Street Address_____
City:_____**State:**_____**Zip Code:**_____
Home Phone:_____**Cell Phone:**_____
Work Phone:_____**Email:**_____
Notes:

Name_____
Street Address_____
City:_____**State:**_____**Zip Code:**_____
Home Phone:_____**Cell Phone:**_____
Work Phone:_____**Email:**_____
Notes:

Name_____
Street Address_____
City:_____**State:**_____**Zip Code:**_____
Home Phone:_____**Cell Phone:**_____
Work Phone:_____**Email:**_____
Notes:

Comments:

Name_____

Street Address_____

City:_____**State:**____**Zip Code:**_____

Home Phone:_____**Cell Phone:**_____

Work Phone:_____**Email:**_____

Notes:

Name_____

Street Address_____

City:_____**State:**____**Zip Code:**_____

Home Phone:_____**Cell Phone:**_____

Work Phone:_____**Email:**_____

Notes:

Name_____

Street Address_____

City:_____**State:**____**Zip Code:**_____

Home Phone:_____**Cell Phone:**_____

Work Phone:_____**Email:**_____

Notes:

Name_____

Street Address_____

City:_____**State:**____**Zip Code:**_____

Home Phone:_____**Cell Phone:**_____

Work Phone:_____**Email:**_____

Notes:

Comments:

Address Book   K

Name_____

Street Address_____

City:_____**State:**____**Zip Code:**_____

Home Phone:_____**Cell Phone:**_____

Work Phone:_____**Email:**_____

Notes:

Name_____

Street Address_____

City:_____**State:**____**Zip Code:**_____

Home Phone:_____**Cell Phone:**_____

Work Phone:_____**Email:**_____

Notes:

Name_____

Street Address_____

City:_____**State:**____**Zip Code:**_____

Home Phone:_____**Cell Phone:**_____

Work Phone:_____**Email:**_____

Notes:

Name_____

Street Address_____

City:_____**State:**____**Zip Code:**_____

Home Phone:_____**Cell Phone:**_____

Work Phone:_____**Email:**_____

Notes:

Comments:

L   **Address Book**

Name_____
Street Address_____
City:_____ **State:**____ **Zip Code:**_____
Home Phone:_____ **Cell Phone:**_____
Work Phone:_____ **Email:**_____
Notes:

Name_____
Street Address_____
City:_____ **State:**____ **Zip Code:**_____
Home Phone:_____ **Cell Phone:**_____
Work Phone:_____ **Email:**_____
Notes:

Name_____
Street Address_____
City:_____ **State:**____ **Zip Code:**_____
Home Phone:_____ **Cell Phone:**_____
Work Phone:_____ **Email:**_____
Notes:

Name_____
Street Address_____
City:_____ **State:**____ **Zip Code:**_____
Home Phone:_____ **Cell Phone:**_____
Work Phone:_____ **Email:**_____
Notes:

Comments:

Address Book   L

Name_____

Street Address_____

City:_____**State:**____**Zip Code:**_____

Home Phone:_____**Cell Phone:**_____

Work Phone:_____**Email:**_____

Notes:

Name_____

Street Address_____

City:_____**State:**____**Zip Code:**_____

Home Phone:_____**Cell Phone:**_____

Work Phone:_____**Email:**_____

Notes:

Name_____

Street Address_____

City:_____**State:**____**Zip Code:**_____

Home Phone:_____**Cell Phone:**_____

Work Phone:_____**Email:**_____

Notes:

Name_____

Street Address_____

City:_____**State:**____**Zip Code:**_____

Home Phone:_____**Cell Phone:**_____

Work Phone:_____**Email:**_____

Notes:

Comments:

Name_____

Street Address_____

City:_____**State:**____**Zip Code:**_____

Home Phone:_____**Cell Phone:**_____

Work Phone:_____**Email:**_____

Notes:

Name_____

Street Address_____

City:_____**State:**____**Zip Code:**_____

Home Phone:_____**Cell Phone:**_____

Work Phone:_____**Email:**_____

Notes:

Name_____

Street Address_____

City:_____**State:**____**Zip Code:**_____

Home Phone:_____**Cell Phone:**_____

Work Phone:_____**Email:**_____

Notes:

Name_____

Street Address_____

City:_____**State:**____**Zip Code:**_____

Home Phone:_____**Cell Phone:**_____

Work Phone:_____**Email:**_____

Notes:

Comments:

Address Book
L

Name_____

Street Address_____

City:_____**State:**____**Zip Code:**_____

Home Phone:_____**Cell Phone:**_____

Work Phone:_____**Email:**_____

Notes:

Name_____

Street Address_____

City:_____**State:**____**Zip Code:**_____

Home Phone:_____**Cell Phone:**_____

Work Phone:_____**Email:**_____

Notes:

Name_____

Street Address_____

City:_____**State:**____**Zip Code:**_____

Home Phone:_____**Cell Phone:**_____

Work Phone:_____**Email:**_____

Notes:

Name_____

Street Address_____

City:_____**State:**____**Zip Code:**_____

Home Phone:_____**Cell Phone:**_____

Work Phone:_____**Email:**_____

Notes:

Comments:

Name_____
Street Address_____
City:_____**State:**____**Zip Code:**_____
Home Phone:_____**Cell Phone:**_____
Work Phone:_____**Email:**_____
Notes:

Name_____
Street Address_____
City:_____**State:**____**Zip Code:**_____
Home Phone:_____**Cell Phone:**_____
Work Phone:_____**Email:**_____
Notes:

Name_____
Street Address_____
City:_____**State:**____**Zip Code:**_____
Home Phone:_____**Cell Phone:**_____
Work Phone:_____**Email:**_____
Notes:

Name_____
Street Address_____
City:_____**State:**____**Zip Code:**_____
Home Phone:_____**Cell Phone:**_____
Work Phone:_____**Email:**_____
Notes:

Comments:

Address Book   M

Name_____

Street Address_____

City:_____State:____Zip Code:_____

Home Phone:_____Cell Phone:_____

Work Phone:_____Email:_____

Notes:

Name_____

Street Address_____

City:_____State:____Zip Code:_____

Home Phone:_____Cell Phone:_____

Work Phone:_____Email:_____

Notes:

Name_____

Street Address_____

City:_____State:____Zip Code:_____

Home Phone:_____Cell Phone:_____

Work Phone:_____Email:_____

Notes:

Name_____

Street Address_____

City:_____State:____Zip Code:_____

Home Phone:_____Cell Phone:_____

Work Phone:_____Email:_____

Notes:

Comments:

M   **Address Book**

Name_____
Street Address_____
City:_____**State:**____**Zip Code:**____
Home Phone:_____**Cell Phone:**_____
Work Phone:_____**Email:**_____
Notes:

Name_____
Street Address_____
City:_____**State:**____**Zip Code:**____
Home Phone:_____**Cell Phone:**_____
Work Phone:_____**Email:**_____
Notes:

Name_____
Street Address_____
City:_____**State:**____**Zip Code:**____
Home Phone:_____**Cell Phone:**_____
Work Phone:_____**Email:**_____
Notes:

Name_____
Street Address_____
City:_____**State:**____**Zip Code:**____
Home Phone:_____**Cell Phone:**_____
Work Phone:_____**Email:**_____
Notes:

Comments:

Address Book   M

Name_____

Street Address_____

City:_____**State:**____**Zip Code:**_____

Home Phone:_____**Cell Phone:**_____

Work Phone:_____**Email:**_____

Notes:

Name_____

Street Address_____

City:_____**State:**____**Zip Code:**_____

Home Phone:_____**Cell Phone:**_____

Work Phone:_____**Email:**_____

Notes:

Name_____

Street Address_____

City:_____**State:**____**Zip Code:**_____

Home Phone:_____**Cell Phone:**_____

Work Phone:_____**Email:**_____

Notes:

Name_____

Street Address_____

City:_____**State:**____**Zip Code:**_____

Home Phone:_____**Cell Phone:**_____

Work Phone:_____**Email:**_____

Notes:

Comments:

Name_____

Street Address_____

City:_____**State:**____**Zip Code:**_____

Home Phone:_____**Cell Phone:**_____

Work Phone:_____**Email:**_____

Notes:

Name_____

Street Address_____

City:_____**State:**____**Zip Code:**_____

Home Phone:_____**Cell Phone:**_____

Work Phone:_____**Email:**_____

Notes:

Name_____

Street Address_____

City:_____**State:**____**Zip Code:**_____

Home Phone:_____**Cell Phone:**_____

Work Phone:_____**Email:**_____

Notes:

Name_____

Street Address_____

City:_____**State:**____**Zip Code:**_____

Home Phone:_____**Cell Phone:**_____

Work Phone:_____**Email:**_____

Notes:

Comments:

Name_____
Street Address_____
City:_____**State:**_____**Zip Code:**_____
Home Phone:_____**Cell Phone:**_____
Work Phone:_____**Email:**_____
Notes:

Name_____
Street Address_____
City:_____**State:**_____**Zip Code:**_____
Home Phone:_____**Cell Phone:**_____
Work Phone:_____**Email:**_____
Notes:

Name_____
Street Address_____
City:_____**State:**_____**Zip Code:**_____
Home Phone:_____**Cell Phone:**_____
Work Phone:_____**Email:**_____
Notes:

Name_____
Street Address_____
City:_____**State:**_____**Zip Code:**_____
Home Phone:_____**Cell Phone:**_____
Work Phone:_____**Email:**_____
Notes:

Comments:

Name_____

Street Address_____

City:_____**State:**____**Zip Code:**_____

Home Phone:_____**Cell Phone:**_____

Work Phone:_____**Email:**_____

Notes:

Name_____

Street Address_____

City:_____**State:**____**Zip Code:**_____

Home Phone:_____**Cell Phone:**_____

Work Phone:_____**Email:**_____

Notes:

Name_____

Street Address_____

City:_____**State:**____**Zip Code:**_____

Home Phone:_____**Cell Phone:**_____

Work Phone:_____**Email:**_____

Notes:

Name_____

Street Address_____

City:_____**State:**____**Zip Code:**_____

Home Phone:_____**Cell Phone:**_____

Work Phone:_____**Email:**_____

Notes:

Comments:

Name_____

Street Address_____

City:_____**State:**____**Zip Code:**_____

Home Phone:_____**Cell Phone:**_____

Work Phone:_____**Email:**_____

Notes:

Name_____

Street Address_____

City:_____**State:**____**Zip Code:**_____

Home Phone:_____**Cell Phone:**_____

Work Phone:_____**Email:**_____

Notes:

Name_____

Street Address_____

City:_____**State:**____**Zip Code:**_____

Home Phone:_____**Cell Phone:**_____

Work Phone:_____**Email:**_____

Notes:

Name_____

Street Address_____

City:_____**State:**____**Zip Code:**_____

Home Phone:_____**Cell Phone:**_____

Work Phone:_____**Email:**_____

Notes:

Comments:

O	Address Book

Name_____

Street Address_____

City:_____**State:**____**Zip Code:**_____

Home Phone:_____**Cell Phone:**_____

Work Phone:_____**Email:**_____

Notes:

Name_____

Street Address_____

City:_____**State:**____**Zip Code:**_____

Home Phone:_____**Cell Phone:**_____

Work Phone:_____**Email:**_____

Notes:

Name_____

Street Address_____

City:_____**State:**____**Zip Code:**_____

Home Phone:_____**Cell Phone:**_____

Work Phone:_____**Email:**_____

Notes:

Name_____

Street Address_____

City:_____**State:**____**Zip Code:**_____

Home Phone:_____**Cell Phone:**_____

Work Phone:_____**Email:**_____

Notes:

Comments:

Address Book O

Name_____

Street Address_____

City:_____State:____Zip Code:_____

Home Phone:_____Cell Phone:_____

Work Phone:_____Email:_____

Notes:

Name_____

Street Address_____

City:_____State:____Zip Code:_____

Home Phone:_____Cell Phone:_____

Work Phone:_____Email:_____

Notes:

Name_____

Street Address_____

City:_____State:____Zip Code:_____

Home Phone:_____Cell Phone:_____

Work Phone:_____Email:_____

Notes:

Name_____

Street Address_____

City:_____State:____Zip Code:_____

Home Phone:_____Cell Phone:_____

Work Phone:_____Email:_____

Notes:

Comments:

Name_____

Street Address_____

City:_____**State:**_____**Zip Code:**_____

Home Phone:_____**Cell Phone:**_____

Work Phone:_____**Email:**_____

Notes:

Name_____

Street Address_____

City:_____**State:**_____**Zip Code:**_____

Home Phone:_____**Cell Phone:**_____

Work Phone:_____**Email:**_____

Notes:

Name_____

Street Address_____

City:_____**State:**_____**Zip Code:**_____

Home Phone:_____**Cell Phone:**_____

Work Phone:_____**Email:**_____

Notes:

Name_____

Street Address_____

City:_____**State:**_____**Zip Code:**_____

Home Phone:_____**Cell Phone:**_____

Work Phone:_____**Email:**_____

Notes:

Comments:

Address Book   O

Name_____

Street Address_____

City:_____**State:**_____**Zip Code:**_____

Home Phone:_____**Cell Phone:**_____

Work Phone:_____**Email:**_____

Notes:

Name_____

Street Address_____

City:_____**State:**_____**Zip Code:**_____

Home Phone:_____**Cell Phone:**_____

Work Phone:_____**Email:**_____

Notes:

Name_____

Street Address_____

City:_____**State:**_____**Zip Code:**_____

Home Phone:_____**Cell Phone:**_____

Work Phone:_____**Email:**_____

Notes:

Name_____

Street Address_____

City:_____**State:**_____**Zip Code:**_____

Home Phone:_____**Cell Phone:**_____

Work Phone:_____**Email:**_____

Notes:

Comments:

Name_____

Street Address_____

City:_____**State:**_____**Zip Code:**_____

Home Phone:_____**Cell Phone:**_____

Work Phone:_____**Email:**_____

Notes:

Name_____

Street Address_____

City:_____**State:**_____**Zip Code:**_____

Home Phone:_____**Cell Phone:**_____

Work Phone:_____**Email:**_____

Notes:

Name_____

Street Address_____

City:_____**State:**_____**Zip Code:**_____

Home Phone:_____**Cell Phone:**_____

Work Phone:_____**Email:**_____

Notes:

Name_____

Street Address_____

City:_____**State:**_____**Zip Code:**_____

Home Phone:_____**Cell Phone:**_____

Work Phone:_____**Email:**_____

Notes:

Comments:

Address Book

Name_____
Street Address_____
City:_____State:____Zip Code:_____
Home Phone:_____Cell Phone:_____
Work Phone:_____Email:_____
Notes:

Name_____
Street Address_____
City:_____State:____Zip Code:_____
Home Phone:_____Cell Phone:_____
Work Phone:_____Email:_____
Notes:

Name_____
Street Address_____
City:_____State:____Zip Code:_____
Home Phone:_____Cell Phone:_____
Work Phone:_____Email:_____
Notes:

Name_____
Street Address_____
City:_____State:____Zip Code:_____
Home Phone:_____Cell Phone:_____
Work Phone:_____Email:_____
Notes:

Comments:

Name_____

Street Address_____

City:_____**State:**____**Zip Code:**_____

Home Phone:_____**Cell Phone:**_____

Work Phone:_____**Email:**_____

Notes:

Name_____

Street Address_____

City:_____**State:**____**Zip Code:**_____

Home Phone:_____**Cell Phone:**_____

Work Phone:_____**Email:**_____

Notes:

Name_____

Street Address_____

City:_____**State:**____**Zip Code:**_____

Home Phone:_____**Cell Phone:**_____

Work Phone:_____**Email:**_____

Notes:

Name_____

Street Address_____

City:_____**State:**____**Zip Code:**_____

Home Phone:_____**Cell Phone:**_____

Work Phone:_____**Email:**_____

Notes:

Comments:

Address Book   P

Name_____
Street Address_____
City:_____**State:**____**Zip Code:**_____
Home Phone:_____**Cell Phone:**_____
Work Phone:_____**Email:**_____
Notes:

Name_____
Street Address_____
City:_____**State:**____**Zip Code:**_____
Home Phone:_____**Cell Phone:**_____
Work Phone:_____**Email:**_____
Notes:

Name_____
Street Address_____
City:_____**State:**____**Zip Code:**_____
Home Phone:_____**Cell Phone:**_____
Work Phone:_____**Email:**_____
Notes:

Name_____
Street Address_____
City:_____**State:**____**Zip Code:**_____
Home Phone:_____**Cell Phone:**_____
Work Phone:_____**Email:**_____
Notes:

Comments:

Address Book

Name_____

Street Address_____

City:_____**State:**____**Zip Code:**_____

Home Phone:_____**Cell Phone:**_____

Work Phone:_____**Email:**_____

Notes:

Name_____

Street Address_____

City:_____**State:**____**Zip Code:**_____

Home Phone:_____**Cell Phone:**_____

Work Phone:_____**Email:**_____

Notes:

Name_____

Street Address_____

City:_____**State:**____**Zip Code:**_____

Home Phone:_____**Cell Phone:**_____

Work Phone:_____**Email:**_____

Notes:

Name_____

Street Address_____

City:_____**State:**____**Zip Code:**_____

Home Phone:_____**Cell Phone:**_____

Work Phone:_____**Email:**_____

Notes:

Comments:

Address Book   Q

Name_____
Street Address_____
City:_____State:____Zip Code:_____
Home Phone:_____Cell Phone:_____
Work Phone:_____Email:_____
Notes:

Name_____
Street Address_____
City:_____State:____Zip Code:_____
Home Phone:_____Cell Phone:_____
Work Phone:_____Email:_____
Notes:

Name_____
Street Address_____
City:_____State:____Zip Code:_____
Home Phone:_____Cell Phone:_____
Work Phone:_____Email:_____
Notes:

Name_____
Street Address_____
City:_____State:____Zip Code:_____
Home Phone:_____Cell Phone:_____
Work Phone:_____Email:_____
Notes:

Comments:

R   **Address Book**

Name_____

Street Address_____

City:_____**State:**____**Zip Code:**_____

Home Phone:_____**Cell Phone:**_____

Work Phone:_____**Email:**_____

Notes:

Name_____

Street Address_____

City:_____**State:**____**Zip Code:**_____

Home Phone:_____**Cell Phone:**_____

Work Phone:_____**Email:**_____

Notes:

Name_____

Street Address_____

City:_____**State:**____**Zip Code:**_____

Home Phone:_____**Cell Phone:**_____

Work Phone:_____**Email:**_____

Notes:

Name_____

Street Address_____

City:_____**State:**____**Zip Code:**_____

Home Phone:_____**Cell Phone:**_____

Work Phone:_____**Email:**_____

Notes:

Comments:

Address Book

Name_____
Street Address_____
City:_____**State:**____**Zip Code:**_____
Home Phone:_____**Cell Phone:**_____
Work Phone:_____**Email:**_____
Notes:

Name_____
Street Address_____
City:_____**State:**____**Zip Code:**_____
Home Phone:_____**Cell Phone:**_____
Work Phone:_____**Email:**_____
Notes:

Name_____
Street Address_____
City:_____**State:**____**Zip Code:**_____
Home Phone:_____**Cell Phone:**_____
Work Phone:_____**Email:**_____
Notes:

Name_____
Street Address_____
City:_____**State:**____**Zip Code:**_____
Home Phone:_____**Cell Phone:**_____
Work Phone:_____**Email:**_____
Notes:

Comments:

Name_____
Street Address_____
City:_____**State:**____**Zip Code:**_____
Home Phone:_____**Cell Phone:**_____
Work Phone:_____**Email:**_____
Notes:

Name_____
Street Address_____
City:_____**State:**____**Zip Code:**_____
Home Phone:_____**Cell Phone:**_____
Work Phone:_____**Email:**_____
Notes:

Name_____
Street Address_____
City:_____**State:**____**Zip Code:**_____
Home Phone:_____**Cell Phone:**_____
Work Phone:_____**Email:**_____
Notes:

Name_____
Street Address_____
City:_____**State:**____**Zip Code:**_____
Home Phone:_____**Cell Phone:**_____
Work Phone:_____**Email:**_____
Notes:

Comments:

Address Book   R

Name_____
Street Address_____
City:_____State:____Zip Code:_____
Home Phone:_____Cell Phone:_____
Work Phone:_____Email:_____
Notes:

Name_____
Street Address_____
City:_____State:____Zip Code:_____
Home Phone:_____Cell Phone:_____
Work Phone:_____Email:_____
Notes:

Name_____
Street Address_____
City:_____State:____Zip Code:_____
Home Phone:_____Cell Phone:_____
Work Phone:_____Email:_____
Notes:

Name_____
Street Address_____
City:_____State:____Zip Code:_____
Home Phone:_____Cell Phone:_____
Work Phone:_____Email:_____
Notes:

Comments:

Name_____

Street Address_____

City:_____**State:**____**Zip Code:**_____

Home Phone:_____**Cell Phone:**_____

Work Phone:_____**Email:**_____

Notes:

Name_____

Street Address_____

City:_____**State:**____**Zip Code:**_____

Home Phone:_____**Cell Phone:**_____

Work Phone:_____**Email:**_____

Notes:

Name_____

Street Address_____

City:_____**State:**____**Zip Code:**_____

Home Phone:_____**Cell Phone:**_____

Work Phone:_____**Email:**_____

Notes:

Name_____

Street Address_____

City:_____**State:**____**Zip Code:**_____

Home Phone:_____**Cell Phone:**_____

Work Phone:_____**Email:**_____

Notes:

Comments:

Address Book   S

Name_____

Street Address_____

City:_____**State:**____**Zip Code:**_____

Home Phone:_____**Cell Phone:**_____

Work Phone:_____**Email:**_____

Notes:

Name_____

Street Address_____

City:_____**State:**____**Zip Code:**_____

Home Phone:_____**Cell Phone:**_____

Work Phone:_____**Email:**_____

Notes:

Name_____

Street Address_____

City:_____**State:**____**Zip Code:**_____

Home Phone:_____**Cell Phone:**_____

Work Phone:_____**Email:**_____

Notes:

Name_____

Street Address_____

City:_____**State:**____**Zip Code:**_____

Home Phone:_____**Cell Phone:**_____

Work Phone:_____**Email:**_____

Notes:

Comments:

Name_____

Street Address_____

City:_____**State:**_____**Zip Code:**_____

Home Phone:_____**Cell Phone:**_____

Work Phone:_____**Email:**_____

Notes:

Name_____

Street Address_____

City:_____**State:**_____**Zip Code:**_____

Home Phone:_____**Cell Phone:**_____

Work Phone:_____**Email:**_____

Notes:

Name_____

Street Address_____

City:_____**State:**_____**Zip Code:**_____

Home Phone:_____**Cell Phone:**_____

Work Phone:_____**Email:**_____

Notes:

Name_____

Street Address_____

City:_____**State:**_____**Zip Code:**_____

Home Phone:_____**Cell Phone:**_____

Work Phone:_____**Email:**_____

Notes:

Comments:

| Address Book | S |

Name_____

Street Address_____

City:_____**State:**____**Zip Code:**_____

Home Phone:_____**Cell Phone:**_____

Work Phone:_____**Email:**_____

Notes:

Name_____

Street Address_____

City:_____**State:**____**Zip Code:**_____

Home Phone:_____**Cell Phone:**_____

Work Phone:_____**Email:**_____

Notes:

Name_____

Street Address_____

City:_____**State:**____**Zip Code:**_____

Home Phone:_____**Cell Phone:**_____

Work Phone:_____**Email:**_____

Notes:

Name_____

Street Address_____

City:_____**State:**____**Zip Code:**_____

Home Phone:_____**Cell Phone:**_____

Work Phone:_____**Email:**_____

Notes:

Comments:

Name_____

Street Address_____

City:_____**State:**____**Zip Code:**_____

Home Phone:_____**Cell Phone:**_____

Work Phone:_____**Email:**_____

Notes:

Name_____

Street Address_____

City:_____**State:**____**Zip Code:**_____

Home Phone:_____**Cell Phone:**_____

Work Phone:_____**Email:**_____

Notes:

Name_____

Street Address_____

City:_____**State:**____**Zip Code:**_____

Home Phone:_____**Cell Phone:**_____

Work Phone:_____**Email:**_____

Notes:

Name_____

Street Address_____

City:_____**State:**____**Zip Code:**_____

Home Phone:_____**Cell Phone:**_____

Work Phone:_____**Email:**_____

Notes:

Comments:

Address Book   T

Name_____

Street Address_____

City:_____**State:**____**Zip Code:**____

Home Phone:_____**Cell Phone:**_____

Work Phone:_____**Email:**_____

Notes:

Name_____

Street Address_____

City:_____**State:**____**Zip Code:**____

Home Phone:_____**Cell Phone:**_____

Work Phone:_____**Email:**_____

Notes:

Name_____

Street Address_____

City:_____**State:**____**Zip Code:**____

Home Phone:_____**Cell Phone:**_____

Work Phone:_____**Email:**_____

Notes:

Name_____

Street Address_____

City:_____**State:**____**Zip Code:**____

Home Phone:_____**Cell Phone:**_____

Work Phone:_____**Email:**_____

Notes:

Comments:

Name_____

Street Address_____

City:_____**State:**____**Zip Code:**_____

Home Phone:_____**Cell Phone:**_____

Work Phone:_____**Email:**_____

Notes:

Name_____

Street Address_____

City:_____**State:**____**Zip Code:**_____

Home Phone:_____**Cell Phone:**_____

Work Phone:_____**Email:**_____

Notes:

Name_____

Street Address_____

City:_____**State:**____**Zip Code:**_____

Home Phone:_____**Cell Phone:**_____

Work Phone:_____**Email:**_____

Notes:

Name_____

Street Address_____

City:_____**State:**____**Zip Code:**_____

Home Phone:_____**Cell Phone:**_____

Work Phone:_____**Email:**_____

Notes:

Comments:

| Address Book | | T |

Name_____
Street Address_____
City:_____**State:**____**Zip Code:**_____
Home Phone:_____**Cell Phone:**_____
Work Phone:_____**Email:**_____
Notes:

Name_____
Street Address_____
City:_____**State:**____**Zip Code:**_____
Home Phone:_____**Cell Phone:**_____
Work Phone:_____**Email:**_____
Notes:

Name_____
Street Address_____
City:_____**State:**____**Zip Code:**_____
Home Phone:_____**Cell Phone:**_____
Work Phone:_____**Email:**_____
Notes:

Name_____
Street Address_____
City:_____**State:**____**Zip Code:**_____
Home Phone:_____**Cell Phone:**_____
Work Phone:_____**Email:**_____
Notes:

Comments:

Name_____
Street Address_____
City:_____**State:**____**Zip Code:**_____
Home Phone:_____**Cell Phone:**_____
Work Phone:_____**Email:**_____
Notes:

Name_____
Street Address_____
City:_____**State:**____**Zip Code:**_____
Home Phone:_____**Cell Phone:**_____
Work Phone:_____**Email:**_____
Notes:

Name_____
Street Address_____
City:_____**State:**____**Zip Code:**_____
Home Phone:_____**Cell Phone:**_____
Work Phone:_____**Email:**_____
Notes:

Name_____
Street Address_____
City:_____**State:**____**Zip Code:**_____
Home Phone:_____**Cell Phone:**_____
Work Phone:_____**Email:**_____
Notes:

Comments:

Address Book U

Name_____

Street Address_____

City:_____**State:**____**Zip Code:**_____

Home Phone:_____**Cell Phone:**_____

Work Phone:_____**Email:**_____

Notes:

Name_____

Street Address_____

City:_____**State:**____**Zip Code:**_____

Home Phone:_____**Cell Phone:**_____

Work Phone:_____**Email:**_____

Notes:

Name_____

Street Address_____

City:_____**State:**____**Zip Code:**_____

Home Phone:_____**Cell Phone:**_____

Work Phone:_____**Email:**_____

Notes:

Name_____

Street Address_____

City:_____**State:**____**Zip Code:**_____

Home Phone:_____**Cell Phone:**_____

Work Phone:_____**Email:**_____

Notes:

Comments:

Name_____

Street Address_____

City:_____**State:**_____**Zip Code:**_____

Home Phone:_____**Cell Phone:**_____

Work Phone:_____**Email:**_____

Notes:

Name_____

Street Address_____

City:_____**State:**_____**Zip Code:**_____

Home Phone:_____**Cell Phone:**_____

Work Phone:_____**Email:**_____

Notes:

Name_____

Street Address_____

City:_____**State:**_____**Zip Code:**_____

Home Phone:_____**Cell Phone:**_____

Work Phone:_____**Email:**_____

Notes:

Name_____

Street Address_____

City:_____**State:**_____**Zip Code:**_____

Home Phone:_____**Cell Phone:**_____

Work Phone:_____**Email:**_____

Notes:

Comments:

Address Book

Name_____
Street Address_____
City:_____State:____Zip Code:_____
Home Phone:_____Cell Phone:_____
Work Phone:_____Email:_____
Notes:

Name_____
Street Address_____
City:_____State:____Zip Code:_____
Home Phone:_____Cell Phone:_____
Work Phone:_____Email:_____
Notes:

Name_____
Street Address_____
City:_____State:____Zip Code:_____
Home Phone:_____Cell Phone:_____
Work Phone:_____Email:_____
Notes:

Name_____
Street Address_____
City:_____State:____Zip Code:_____
Home Phone:_____Cell Phone:_____
Work Phone:_____Email:_____
Notes:

Comments:

Name_____
Street Address_____
City:_____**State:**____**Zip Code:**_____
Home Phone:_____**Cell Phone:**_____
Work Phone:_____**Email:**_____
Notes:

Name_____
Street Address_____
City:_____**State:**____**Zip Code:**_____
Home Phone:_____**Cell Phone:**_____
Work Phone:_____**Email:**_____
Notes:

Name_____
Street Address_____
City:_____**State:**____**Zip Code:**_____
Home Phone:_____**Cell Phone:**_____
Work Phone:_____**Email:**_____
Notes:

Name_____
Street Address_____
City:_____**State:**____**Zip Code:**_____
Home Phone:_____**Cell Phone:**_____
Work Phone:_____**Email:**_____
Notes:

Comments:

Name_____

Street Address_____

City:_____**State:**____**Zip Code:**_____

Home Phone:_____**Cell Phone:**_____

Work Phone:_____**Email:**_____

Notes:

Name_____

Street Address_____

City:_____**State:**____**Zip Code:**_____

Home Phone:_____**Cell Phone:**_____

Work Phone:_____**Email:**_____

Notes:

Name_____

Street Address_____

City:_____**State:**____**Zip Code:**_____

Home Phone:_____**Cell Phone:**_____

Work Phone:_____**Email:**_____

Notes:

Name_____

Street Address_____

City:_____**State:**____**Zip Code:**_____

Home Phone:_____**Cell Phone:**_____

Work Phone:_____**Email:**_____

Notes:

Comments:

Name_____
Street Address_____
City:_____**State:**____**Zip Code:**_____
Home Phone:_____**Cell Phone:**_____
Work Phone:_____**Email:**_____
Notes:

Name_____
Street Address_____
City:_____**State:**____**Zip Code:**_____
Home Phone:_____**Cell Phone:**_____
Work Phone:_____**Email:**_____
Notes:

Name_____
Street Address_____
City:_____**State:**____**Zip Code:**_____
Home Phone:_____**Cell Phone:**_____
Work Phone:_____**Email:**_____
Notes:

Name_____
Street Address_____
City:_____**State:**____**Zip Code:**_____
Home Phone:_____**Cell Phone:**_____
Work Phone:_____**Email:**_____
Notes:

Comments:

Address Book   V

Name_____

Street Address_____

City:_____State:____Zip Code:_____

Home Phone:_____Cell Phone:_____

Work Phone:_____Email:_____

Notes:

Name_____

Street Address_____

City:_____State:____Zip Code:_____

Home Phone:_____Cell Phone:_____

Work Phone:_____Email:_____

Notes:

Name_____

Street Address_____

City:_____State:____Zip Code:_____

Home Phone:_____Cell Phone:_____

Work Phone:_____Email:_____

Notes:

Name_____

Street Address_____

City:_____State:____Zip Code:_____

Home Phone:_____Cell Phone:_____

Work Phone:_____Email:_____

Notes:

Comments:

Name_____

Street Address_____

City:_____**State:**_____**Zip Code:**_____

Home Phone:_____**Cell Phone:**_____

Work Phone:_____**Email:**_____

Notes:

Name_____

Street Address_____

City:_____**State:**_____**Zip Code:**_____

Home Phone:_____**Cell Phone:**_____

Work Phone:_____**Email:**_____

Notes:

Name_____

Street Address_____

City:_____**State:**_____**Zip Code:**_____

Home Phone:_____**Cell Phone:**_____

Work Phone:_____**Email:**_____

Notes:

Name_____

Street Address_____

City:_____**State:**_____**Zip Code:**_____

Home Phone:_____**Cell Phone:**_____

Work Phone:_____**Email:**_____

Notes:

Comments:

Name_____

Street Address_____

City:_____State:____Zip Code:_____

Home Phone:_____Cell Phone:_____

Work Phone:_____Email:_____

Notes:

Name_____

Street Address_____

City:_____State:____Zip Code:_____

Home Phone:_____Cell Phone:_____

Work Phone:_____Email:_____

Notes:

Name_____

Street Address_____

City:_____State:____Zip Code:_____

Home Phone:_____Cell Phone:_____

Work Phone:_____Email:_____

Notes:

Name_____

Street Address_____

City:_____State:____Zip Code:_____

Home Phone:_____Cell Phone:_____

Work Phone:_____Email:_____

Notes:

Comments:

W	Address Book

Name_____

Street Address_____

City:_____**State:**_____**Zip Code:**_____

Home Phone:_____**Cell Phone:**_____

Work Phone:_____**Email:**_____

Notes:

Name_____

Street Address_____

City:_____**State:**_____**Zip Code:**_____

Home Phone:_____**Cell Phone:**_____

Work Phone:_____**Email:**_____

Notes:

Name_____

Street Address_____

City:_____**State:**_____**Zip Code:**_____

Home Phone:_____**Cell Phone:**_____

Work Phone:_____**Email:**_____

Notes:

Name_____

Street Address_____

City:_____**State:**_____**Zip Code:**_____

Home Phone:_____**Cell Phone:**_____

Work Phone:_____**Email:**_____

Notes:

Comments:

Name_____
Street Address_____
City:_____State:____Zip Code:_____
Home Phone:_____Cell Phone:_____
Work Phone:_____Email:_____
Notes:

Name_____
Street Address_____
City:_____State:____Zip Code:_____
Home Phone:_____Cell Phone:_____
Work Phone:_____Email:_____
Notes:

Name_____
Street Address_____
City:_____State:____Zip Code:_____
Home Phone:_____Cell Phone:_____
Work Phone:_____Email:_____
Notes:

Name_____
Street Address_____
City:_____State:____Zip Code:_____
Home Phone:_____Cell Phone:_____
Work Phone:_____Email:_____
Notes:

Comments:

X	Address Book

Name_____
Street Address_____
City:_____**State:**____**Zip Code:**_____
Home Phone:_____**Cell Phone:**_____
Work Phone:_____**Email:**_____
Notes:

Name_____
Street Address_____
City:_____**State:**____**Zip Code:**_____
Home Phone:_____**Cell Phone:**_____
Work Phone:_____**Email:**_____
Notes:

Name_____
Street Address_____
City:_____**State:**____**Zip Code:**_____
Home Phone:_____**Cell Phone:**_____
Work Phone:_____**Email:**_____
Notes:

Name_____
Street Address_____
City:_____**State:**____**Zip Code:**_____
Home Phone:_____**Cell Phone:**_____
Work Phone:_____**Email:**_____
Notes:

Comments:

Address Book   X

Name_____
Street Address_____
City:_____**State:**____**Zip Code:**_____
Home Phone:_____**Cell Phone:**_____
Work Phone:_____**Email:**_____
Notes:

Name_____
Street Address_____
City:_____**State:**____**Zip Code:**_____
Home Phone:_____**Cell Phone:**_____
Work Phone:_____**Email:**_____
Notes:

Name_____
Street Address_____
City:_____**State:**____**Zip Code:**_____
Home Phone:_____**Cell Phone:**_____
Work Phone:_____**Email:**_____
Notes:

Name_____
Street Address_____
City:_____**State:**____**Zip Code:**_____
Home Phone:_____**Cell Phone:**_____
Work Phone:_____**Email:**_____
Notes:

Comments:

Name_____

Street Address_____

City:_____**State:**____**Zip Code:**_____

Home Phone:_____**Cell Phone:**_____

Work Phone:_____**Email:**_____

Notes:

Name_____

Street Address_____

City:_____**State:**____**Zip Code:**_____

Home Phone:_____**Cell Phone:**_____

Work Phone:_____**Email:**_____

Notes:

Name_____

Street Address_____

City:_____**State:**____**Zip Code:**_____

Home Phone:_____**Cell Phone:**_____

Work Phone:_____**Email:**_____

Notes:

Name_____

Street Address_____

City:_____**State:**____**Zip Code:**_____

Home Phone:_____**Cell Phone:**_____

Work Phone:_____**Email:**_____

Notes:

Comments:

Name_____

Street Address_____

City:_____**State:**____**Zip Code:**_____

Home Phone:_____**Cell Phone:**_____

Work Phone:_____**Email:**_____

Notes:

Name_____

Street Address_____

City:_____**State:**____**Zip Code:**_____

Home Phone:_____**Cell Phone:**_____

Work Phone:_____**Email:**_____

Notes:

Name_____

Street Address_____

City:_____**State:**____**Zip Code:**_____

Home Phone:_____**Cell Phone:**_____

Work Phone:_____**Email:**_____

Notes:

Name_____

Street Address_____

City:_____**State:**____**Zip Code:**_____

Home Phone:_____**Cell Phone:**_____

Work Phone:_____**Email:**_____

Notes:

Comments:

Name_____

Street Address_____

City:_____ **State:**____ **Zip Code:**_____

Home Phone:_____ **Cell Phone:**_____

Work Phone:_____ **Email:**_____

Notes:

Name_____

Street Address_____

City:_____ **State:**____ **Zip Code:**_____

Home Phone:_____ **Cell Phone:**_____

Work Phone:_____ **Email:**_____

Notes:

Name_____

Street Address_____

City:_____ **State:**____ **Zip Code:**_____

Home Phone:_____ **Cell Phone:**_____

Work Phone:_____ **Email:**_____

Notes:

Name_____

Street Address_____

City:_____ **State:**____ **Zip Code:**_____

Home Phone:_____ **Cell Phone:**_____

Work Phone:_____ **Email:**_____

Notes:

Comments:

Address Book   Z

Name_____

Street Address_____

City:_____**State:**____**Zip Code:**_____

Home Phone:_____**Cell Phone:**_____

Work Phone:_____**Email:**_____

Notes:

Name_____

Street Address_____

City:_____**State:**____**Zip Code:**_____

Home Phone:_____**Cell Phone:**_____

Work Phone:_____**Email:**_____

Notes:

Name_____

Street Address_____

City:_____**State:**____**Zip Code:**_____

Home Phone:_____**Cell Phone:**_____

Work Phone:_____**Email:**_____

Notes:

Name_____

Street Address_____

City:_____**State:**____**Zip Code:**_____

Home Phone:_____**Cell Phone:**_____

Work Phone:_____**Email:**_____

Notes:

Comments:

PASSWORD LIST

WEBSITE/ PROGRAM	USER NAME	PASSWORD

PASSWORD LIST

WEBSITE/ PROGRAM	USER NAME	PASSWORD

PASSWORD LIST

WEBSITE/ PROGRAM	USER NAME	PASSWORD

PASSWORD LIST

WEBSITE/ PROGRAM	USER NAME	PASSWORD

PASSWORD LIST

WEBSITE/ PROGRAM	USER NAME	PASSWORD

PASSWORD LIST

WEBSITE/ PROGRAM	USER NAME	PASSWORD

PASSWORD LIST

WEBSITE/ PROGRAM	USER NAME	PASSWORD

PASSWORD LIST

WEBSITE/ PROGRAM	USER NAME	PASSWORD

BIRTHDAY/ANNIVERSARY

JANUARY

NAME	Birthday Date	Anniversary Date

BIRTHDAY/ANNIVERSARY

FEBRUARY

NAME	Birthday Date	Anniversary Date

BIRTHDAY/ANNIVERSARY

MARCH

NAME	Birthday Date	Anniversary Date

BIRTHDAY/ANNIVERSARY

APRIL

NAME	Birthday Date	Anniversary Date

BIRTHDAY/ANNIVERSARY

MAY

NAME	Birthday Date	Anniversary Date

BIRTHDAY/ANNIVERSARY

JUNE

NAME	Birthday Date	Anniversary Date

BIRTHDAY/ANNIVERSARY

JULY

NAME	Birthday Date	Anniversary Date

BIRTHDAY/ANNIVERSARY

AUGUST

NAME	Birthday Date	Anniversary Date

BIRTHDAY/ANNIVERSARY

SEPTEMBER

NAME	Birthday Date	Anniversary Date

BIRTHDAY/ANNIVERSARY

OCTOBER

NAME	Birthday Date	Anniversary Date

BIRTHDAY/ANNIVERSARY

NOVEMBER

NAME	Birthday Date	Anniversary Date

BIRTHDAY/ANNIVERSARY

DECEMBER

NAME	Birthday Date	Anniversary Date